Kinghorn Loch  a very varied c

Birds come a ns, but there is st whether you a or just a casual o

If you are very patient and lucky you may see a beautiful kingfisher looking for food or spot our resident Water Rail skulking around the ponds at the Bird Hide.

Spring is a busy time with lots of nesting birds. Observe the Great Crested Grebe and their remarkable courtship display and the Mallard ducks and Coots with their many chicks. The Swans chasing intruders.

The surrounding woodlands are home to many species going about their daily business. Blue Tits, Coal Tits, Great Tits and Loch Tailed tits reside in the woodlands together with Goldfinch, Goldcrest, Linnets and many more.

This booklet is a simple guide to help both adults and children alike identify the many species resident in this beautiful landscape in the changing seasons.

I would like to thank Danny Wallace for his time consuming work recording these birds and for the many lovely photographs supplied by Danny Wallace, Drew Wallace, Roy Balfour and William Dickson.

My sincere thanks go to the **Fife Environment Trust and Awards for All** for funding the printing of this booklet.

The booklet is free and the publication is not for profit, however donations would be appreciated. I hope you will find it useful in identifying the many birds in and around the loch area.

This is the second edition of the booklet, the first having been published in 2011. This is a new revised addition with many new photographs.

Swallow chicks in nest

Blackbird
A well loved song bird. The male bird is black with a distinctive orange beak whilst the female is brown.

Blackcap
The male's black and female's brown crown distinguish it from all other warblers. Song a musical, high pitched, rather staccato warble.

Black-head Gull
Generally the most frequently seen gull inland. The dark brown hood of the breeding plumage, white blaze on forewing and red bill and legs are distinctive.

Blue Tit
One of the commonest tits and with a substantial amount of blue in its plumage. Likes to nest in a hole in a tree and readily takes to nest boxes.

Bullfinch

A very distinctive bird with its black crown, rosy breast and cheeks and white rump. Females are similar but duller. Likes to eat fruit buds.

Buzzard

The most common large bird of prey. It soars overhead with broad wings in a leisurely fashion uttering a loud gull like *pee-oo* cry.

Canada Goose

The largest of our three black-necked geese and likely to be seen inland. A long established introduction from North America, it now breeds widely by freshwater throughout Great Britain. Its call is a loud double trumpeting *ker Konk*. We have one permanent resident at loch usually seen with the Greylag Geese.

Carrion Crow

A common bird in Britain the all black carrion crow differs from the rook with its feathered face and harsher voice.

Chaffinch

One of our most common birds, breeding in woods, scrub, hedgerows, parks and gardens. The male's handsome plumage is distinctive.

Chiffchaff

One of the earliest migrants to arrive usually in late March. Best distinctions are its monotonous *chiff-chaff* song and call-note *hweet.* More restricted to mature woodland. It appears browner, with less green and yellow in its plumage than a Willow Warbler.

Coat Tit

The smallest British tit, easily identified by the prominent white patch on its nape and also by its high pitched *ticha ticha* call.

Collared Dove

A newcomer, which has only bred in Britain since the 1950's. Larger than the Turtle Dove, with duller grey plumage and more white in the tail and a black neck bar. Song is persistent *coo-cooo-cuh*.

Common Gull

Smaller than a herring gull, but with both bill and legs a greenish yellow. Widespread and common both inland and by the sea. It has a shrill mewing *kee-ya* sound. Breeds mainly in Scotland and Ireland.

Coot

Differs from a moorhen by its white bill and forehead. Aggressive chases are characteristic and it dives readily.

Cormorant

The largest all-dark British seabird, with a white face patch and in the breeding season also white thigh patches.

Can be seen on inland fresh water during the winter.

Dunnock

Also known as a Hedgesparrow, the Dunnock is

a common breeding bird in woodland, scrub, farmland, parks and gardens. Thin bill, grey breast and speckled flanks all distinguish it from the house sparrow. It has a loud *chee-ip* sound along with various chirps and twitters.

Fieldfare

The larger of our two winter visitor thrushes. It has a blue-grey head and rump contrasting with the chestnut back. Widespread throughout Britain especially on farmland with hedges and berry-bearing shrubs Has a harsh repeated *chack-chack*.

Goldeneye

A diving duck recognisable by its peaked head and the drake by its white face-spot. A common winter visitor to both fresh and salt water. Breeds only at one or two places in the Scottish Highlands.

Goldcrest

The smallest British bird. It has a tiny, needle-like bill. The male having an orange and the female a yellow crest. Found mostly wherever there are a few pines, spruces, yews or other conifers.

Goldfinch

Widespread throughout Britain but uncommon in north half of Scotland. Very colourful bird having a unique combination of black, white, red and yellow plumage. Well known for its habit of feeding on thistle seeds.

Great Crested Grebe

Our largest grebe, it is very distinctive in breeding plumage with double horned crests and reddish facial frills used in their remarkable head-wagging courtship display. Nest always over water, often anchored to aquatic vegetation. Female carries chicks on her back.

Great Spotted Woodpecker

The largest of our two black and white woodpeckers and easily recognised by its size, red vent and red nape-patch (absent in the female). It has a curious rattling song, made by pecking vigorously at resonant dry wood.

Great Tit

The largest in the tit family being the size of a sparrow. Recognised by its white cheeks on a black head and broad, black bib running down a yellow breast.

Greenfinch

One of the commonest garden birds and also seen flocking with other finches on farmland during the winter. Bright yellow wing patches on a dull greenish yellow plumage.

Grey Heron

The largest long-legged British bird that wades in water. Often seen as a huge, broad-winged bird flapping slowly overhead.

Greylag Goose

A winter visitor it frequents northern farmland and coastal areas. Best distinguished by its pale grey forewing in flight and its combination of orange bill and pink legs. We have a number of permanent residents on the loch.

Grey Wagtail

Blue-grey upperparts, yellowish rump and longer tail distinguish it from the yellow wagtail. It has a shorter higher pitched call than other wagtails.

Herring Gull

A common gull by the sea and also inland. Yellow bill and pink legs distinguish it from the smaller Common Gull. Breeds on sea cliffs and on buildings in seaside towns.

House Martin

Summer visitor which arrives a little later than the swallow, in mid or late April. Distinguished by its white rump, short tail and all-white underparts. Builds a mud nest on buildings or in caves.

Kestrel

Common bird of prey seen in both cities and the countryside. Best know for its habit of hovering in search of prey usually small rodents.

Kingfisher

A beautiful bird, most often seen as a sapphire flash as it speeds down a river or pond. Breeds in holes by or near fresh water.

Lesser Black-backed Gull

Widespread around the coast and breeding mainly on the ground. Both bill and legs yellow in colour.

Linnet

A bird of heaths and scrub, but found in a wide variety of man-made habitats, often breeding in small colonies like the greenfinch. Has a grey head and chestnut back.

Little Grebe

Also known as Dabchick, the Little Grebe is our smallest and commonest grebe. The Little Grebe is an accomplished diver and has a whinnying cry.

Longtailed Tit

A very distinctive small tit, usually seen in groups flying from bush to bush and easily identified by their long tails. Makes a beautifully woven nest from moss and cobwebs.

Magpie

Unmistakable with its long tail and black and white plumage.
Common in farming areas it has a chattering chuckle.

Mallard

The largest and commonest British wild duck both inland and on the coast. Drake has green head, white neck-ring and purple-brown breast. Females are brown with a blue and white bar on their wing.

Moorhen

Easily recognised by its red bill and forehead. Perches in trees and bushes. A very common and widespread waterfowl in Britain.

Mute Swan

The most common swan and recognised by its orange bill and black knob. Nests in a huge pile of vegetation.

Pheasant

A well known game bird, the male bird is very colourful, whereas the female is brown with a shorter tail Prefers to run for cover, but has a noisy take-off when flying. It produces a *karrk-karrk* sound.

Pied Wagtail

Well known for their habit of wagging their tails up and down. This is the only black and white species in Britain and it is widespread and common in all seasons.

Pochard

The male duck has a chestnut head, black breast and grey under parts.

Redwing

The smaller of Britain's two winter visitor thrushes. Recognised by its white eye-stripe and red flanks and under-wing. Often seen with fieldfares.

Reed Bunting

Most often found in reed-beds or by fresh water. Cock has a striking black head-dress and the hen is more sparrow-like but distinguishable by white outer tail feathers. Has a squeaky song.

Robin

One of Britain's best loved birds. Whole face and breast an orange-red. Sings throughout the year.

Rock Dove
The rarest British breeding dove confined to Scottish and Irish coasts. The Rock Dove has white rump, greyish wing-tips and broad black wing-bars.

Scaup
Similar to Tufted duck. The male is grey/black whilst the female has a white facial mark. Breeds beside lochs and rivers. Mostly a winter visitor.

Sedge Warbler
Has a conspicuous white eye-stripe and a varied song, which has more harsh notes than Reed and Marsh Warblers.

Siskin

A small greenish finch. Yellow rump of both sexes and black crown and chin of male are good field marks. Much commoner as a winter visitor.

Skylark

Common throughout Britain and performs a sustained song often from a great height. Generally a streaky brown, slightly crested with white outer tail.

Song Thrush

Common and widespread in gardens, woods, farmland and other open country with trees and bushes. Conspicuously spotted breast and loud, clear, repetitive song.

Sparrowhawk

Combination of long tail, blunt wings and 'flap and glide' flight distinguish it from the Kestrel. Hunts by flying fast usually low amongst woodland or along hedgerows.

Spotted Flycatcher

The upright stance and rapid flights from the same perch after insects identify this bird. Main call a Robin-like *tzee* song. Seen in open woodland. Summer visitor.

Starling

A widespread and common bird. Has striking plumage and a bustling gait. Call a harsh descending *tcheer.* Has a rather warbly song. Good mimic.

Swallow

This summer visitor is identified by its long, forked tail, all blue under parts and chestnut throat and forehead. A highly skilled, graceful and aerobatic flying bird, it normally only settles on the ground to collect nesting material.

Swift

A common summer migrant breeding in crevices in buildings. Long wings, short tail and all-dark plumage. Present mid May to early August.

Treecreeper

The only small land bird with a curved beak and the only one that climbs trees, indeed being hardly ever seen away from tree trunks. Nests in remarkably narrow crevices, often between ivy stems and a tree-trunk.

Tree Sparrow

Different from the House Sparrow in that it has an all-chestnut crown and a black cheek-patch. Nests in small colonies in holes in trees, cliffs and buildings. Habitat is usually woods and areas with mature trees. Has a high-pitched *teck* sound.

Tufted Duck

A common diving duck. The drake has a head-tuft and dark back. Breeds in fresh water throughout Britain.

Water Rail

A shy, skulking bird with a long red bill and barred flanks. Voice very varied, clucking, grunting and squealing.

Whitethroat

The male has a grey cap and cheeks contrasting with a white throat. The female has a white throat under a brown head. Its song is a rapid chattering often delivered during a dancing song flight. Summer visitor breeding throughout Britain and wintering in Africa.

Wigeon

Mainly a winter visitor whose presence can be detected by its characteristic *whee-oo* call. Breeds most commonly in

Scotland. Male's buff cream and chestnut head and grey under- parts are distinctive.

Willow Warbler

Found wherever there are trees or shrubs. Very

like the Chiffchaff but has slightly yellower underparts and usually paler, flesh-coloured legs. Has a *hoo-eet* call.

Woodcock
Like a big, stocky Snipe and usually found in damp woodland. Rises noisily and dodges rapidly away. Breeds throughout Britain. Migrates from the Continent each Autumn.

Woodpigeon

Britain's largest pigeon and regarded as a serious agricultural pest. Voice *Coo-coo-coo*. Has conspicuous white neck patch bordered with glossy green.

Wren

One of Britain's smallest birds and found in a wide range of habitats. It has a warm brown plumage and a habit of cocking up its remarkably short tail. Song is a loud and vigorous burst of clear, trilling notes. It also has a scolding *tic-tic-tic*.

Yellowhammer

Bright yellow bird well known for its monotonous high-pitched song. Females are browner and less yellow. Habitat is farmland, hedgerow, heath and scrub.

Farmyard & Hybrid Geese

Lastly I must mention the noisy white farmyard and hybrid geese who screech at most visitors on arrival. They have been resident for many years and have increased in number having bred successfully over a number of years.